3-

FACTOR WORDS

A Collection of The O'Reilly Factor's
Favorite "Words of the Day"

EXPANDED SECOND EDITION

BY

BILL O'REILLY
AND THE O'REILLY FACTOR STAFF

This book is dedicated to everyone who has helped BillOReilly.com
make millions of dollars in charitable contributions over the years.
The Factor salutes you—each of you is a patriot.

INTRODUCTION

It all began with a teed off Factor viewer who emailed me demanding to know why I used the word 'perspicacious,' and asking what it meant. I read the criticism with an open mind, remembering one of my journalism professors telling me never to use big words on TV because if the audience doesn't know the word's meaning, they'll be angry with you.

But, instead of following the professor's advice, I decided to expand my use of big and obscure words because they're fun. Presto—the Factor's "word of the day" came into being, and here we are with the second edition of "Factor Words," due to an unbelievable amount of demand.

Our research shows the most commonly used words of the day are bloviate, pecksniffian, mendacious, popinjay, blooter, poltroon, blatherskite, jackanapes, and ninnyhammer. All are defined in this volume, plus two hundred forty-one more, fifty of which are new for this edition. All of these words have been used on The Factor at some point in time—some more than once.

Many of these words are "negative," and I still get mail on that as well. "Can't you have some positive words of the day, O'Reilly?" Well, don't be truculent! Negative words are simply more entertaining than positive words. Or maybe I'm just a curmudgeon.

Enjoy this adventure in vocabulary and pass the words along to your kids, grandkids, or some urchin who is annoying you on a plane.

Finally, thanks for buying this book. Your perspicacity is now assured.

FACTOR WORDS

A Collection of The O'Reilly Factor's
Favorite "Words of the Day"

EXPANDED SECOND EDITION

agog

uh-GOG

adj. highly excited by eagerness, curiosity, anticipation

Almost everyone was **agog** when the uninvited couple strolled into the state dinner at the White House.

august

aw-GUST

adj. inspiring admiration or reverence

The ***august*** senator rose from his seat
to give an inspiring speech.

autocratic

aw-tuh-KRAT-ick

adj. acting like someone who has undisputed influence, power or authority

When he expressed an opinion they deemed offensive, his *autocratic* bosses at NPR swung the proverbial axe.

balderdash

BALL-dur-dash

n. senseless, stupid, or exaggerated talk or writing; nonsense

Oh *balderdash*! How can the Speaker of the House claim her excessive use of a taxpayer-funded private jet was to the benefit of the American people?

barbermonger

BAR-bur-mung-ur

n. a vain and superficial man; a fop

The haughty gubernatorial candidate picked a ***barbermonger*** as his running mate.

battology

buh-TOL-uh-gee

n. constant repetition of words in writing or speaking

In a display of **battology** at its most annoying, the environmentalist used the term "climate change" again and again throughout his speech.

bedraggled

bih-DRAG-guld

adj. filthy and limp

When Saddam Hussein was captured by American troops and yanked from his rathole, the once-powerful dictator looked completely *bedraggled*.

bellicose

BELL-uh-kose

adj. aggressively hostile; belligerent; pugnacious

A handful of **bellicose** protesters disrupted the Congressional hearings with their loud shouts and taunts.

bilge

BILJ

n. stupid talk or writing; nonsense

Most arguments against Jessica's Law consisted of unadulterated *bilge*.

bilious

BIL-yus

adj. extremely unpleasant or distasteful

The senator's **bilious** and over-the-top rant against his opponent led voters to reconsider whether he had the composure and class necessary to be commander-in-chief.

blatherskite

BLATH-ur-skite

n. a foolish and overly talkative person

Why did the ***blatherskite*** cross the road?
To drone on and bore more folks on the other side.

blooter

BLOO-tur

n. a fool; an oaf; a blunderer

When writing to The Factor, you will come off as a complete *blooter* if you forget to include your name and town with your correspondence.

bloviate

BLOW-vee-ate

v. to speak pompously

It's better to remain silent and be thought a fool than to **bloviate** and remove all doubt. (With apologies to Honest Abe.)

boorish

BOOR-ish

adj. unmannered; crude; insensitive

Your humble correspondent has been accused of *boorish* behavior, but The Factor's format mandates that guests who attempt to deceive the viewer with spin must be interrupted.

bovine

BOH-vine

adj. stolid; dull

CNN, once the dominant player in cable news, now seems positively ***bovine*** compared to FNC's vibrancy.

braggadocio

brag-uh-DOH-show

n. empty boasting; bragging

It was nothing but ***braggadocio*** when Libyan dictator Moammar Qaddafi insisted his corrupt regime could not possibly be brought down by international forces.

brazen

BRAY-zen

adj. shameless or impudent

She was **brazen** enough to believe she could waltz into the No Spin Zone and get away with dodging questions.

brimborion

brim-BOR-ee-un

n. a worthless object; a trinket

Though plastic beads and faux gemstones may seem like nothing more than ***brimborions*** to most folks, they are invaluable treasures to most little girls.

broozle

BROO-zul

v. to sweat severely

Despite his pitch-perfect performance at the GOP debates, the candidate's propensity to **broozle** was all the post-debate commentators could talk about.

buffoon

buh-FOON

n. person who amuses others with tricks or jokes; undignified joking

Late-night comedians often acted like a bunch of *buffoons* throughout the entire Bush administration, constantly belittling the president and all things conservative.

bulkateer

bulk-uh-TEER

n. a person who overlooks meritorius or valiant behavior

After firefighters rescued her cat from a tree, the **bulkateer** uttered nary a word of thanks.

bumpkin

BUMP-kin

n. an awkward, simple yokel

Secular progressives tend to view religious folks as poor, dumb *bumpkins*.

bumptious

BUMP-shus

adj. offensively self-assertive

Level-headed folks aren't swayed by the ridiculous arguments that *bumptious* 9/11 conspiracy theorists continue to spout.

bunkum

BUNG-kum

n. insincere talk

The word "***bunkum***" is acutally derived from the name of Buncombe County in North Carolina, where a certain politician was infamous for speaking pure twaddle.

cacophonous

kuh-KOFF-uh-nuss

adj. harsh and unpleasant-sounding

The *cacophonous* chorus of Code Pink protesters drowned out rational discussion when they stood up and shouted down the general's Congressional testimony on the war in Afghanistan.

callow

KAL-oh

adj. immature or inexperienced

In America, even the most *callow* small-town boy can grow up to be a famous and humble correspondent.

cantankerous

can-TANK-ur-us

adj. ill-tempered and quarrelsome; disagreeable

The defendant's father took the stand for the prosecution, but his *cantankerous* demeanor led the jury to look at him and his testimony with suspicion.

caperlash

KAY-pur-lash

n. abusive language

Chief Justice John Roberts found himself the target of ideological *caperlash* by those who assumed he'd vote with the court's conservatives on Obamacare.

capricious

kuh-PREE-shus

adj. subject to, led by, or indicative of caprice or whim

Courts have ruled that the death penalty, if applied in a *capricious* and unpredictable manner, violates the Constitution.

captious

KAP-shus

adj. prone to finding faults

Rather than viewing America as a fount of good in the world, many *captious* critics on the left prefer to focus on the country's faults.

caterwauling

KAT-ur-wall-ing

n. a cry or screech like a female cat in heat

Many folks remember unscrupulous televangelists *caterwauling* and crying during their broadcasts as they begged for donations.

caustic

KAW-stick

adj. severely critical or sarcastic

His many *caustic* reviews earned Frank Rich the infamous title of "Butcher of Broadway."

cautel

KAW-tul

n. craftiness; deceit; falsity

Predictably, opinion pieces in liberal newspapers are still accusing President George W. Bush of *cautel* in justifying his decision to go to war.

chameleon

kuh-MEE-lee-un

n. an inconsistent person

The capricious candidate, obviously a political *chameleon*, put forth diametrically opposed positions when speaking to different groups.

charlatan

SHAR-luh-tin

n. a person who claims to have more knowledge or skill than he or she actually possesses

When it comes to politics, there are far too many **charlatans** out there trying to line their own pockets while pretending to be looking out for the folks.

chimera

ky-MEER-uh

n. a grotesque, horrifying monster

Don't mention it to radical feminists, but in Greek mythology, the ***chimera***—a fire-breathing creature that was part goat, part snake, and part lion—was always a female.

choleric

KOLL-ur-ick

adj. irritable, easily angered, hot-tempered

General Patton, known for his *choleric* outbursts, was reprimanded when he slapped a soldier in 1943.

chuffiness

CHUFF-ee-ness

adj. churlishness, boorishness

The gubernatorial candidate approached the situation regarding his allegedly illegal alien employees with a *chuffiness* that was beneath the office he sought.

churlish

CHURL-ish

adj. rude; surly; vulgar

In addition to being incompetent, the tech support guy had the gall to get *churlish* when I asked a question.

clinchpoop

KLINCH-poop

n. a moronic person

A word of warning... don't be a *clinchpoop* and write letters of complaint to The Factor without backing up your beef with solid facts and examples.

codger

KODJ-ur

n. an eccentric man

To qualify as a *codger*, it helps to be elderly and a bit odd, and it's absolutely mandatory to have a "Y" chromosome.

codswallop

CODZ-wol-up

n. nonsense; rubbish

After a careful review of the defense team's arguments, The Factor's legal analysts have concluded that the defendant is guilty and that her insanity plea is *codswallop*.

conniption

cun-NIP-shun

n. a fit of hysterical excitement or anger

The woman seemed quite unstable, having a laughing *conniption* one minute and flying into a *conniption* of rage the next.

contentious

cun-TEN-shus

adj. argumentative; abrasive; quarrelsome

What started as a mere disagreement about a controversy within the Miss USA pageant eventually erupted into a *contentious* war of words between real estate mogul Donald Trump and talk show veteran Rosie O'Donnell.

contumacious

kon-too-MAY-shus

adj. stubbornly perverse;
rebellious; insubordinate

With its insistence on conformity and deference to authority,
the Army is not the best place for a *contumacious* young man.

coxcomb

COX-comb

n. a conceited dandy

Former presidential candidate John Edwards revealed himself to be a true *coxcomb* in the Internet video where he was caught combing his hair to perfection for several minutes.

craven

CRAY-ven

adj. totally without courage, fearful

He was invited on the show to defend his position, but the *craven* politician elected to hide under his desk.

cretin

KREE-tin

n. a stupid, obtuse, or mentally defective person

The BP CEO's weekend sailing trip during the oil spill crisis sparked anger and made him look like an apathetic *cretin*.

crosspatch

CROSS-patch

n. a crabby or ill-tempered person

There seems to be a mate for just about everyone, even the most disagreeable *crosspatch*.

curmudgeon

ker-MUHJ-un

n. a cranky, disagreeable and stubborn person

The peevish economist was known to be a disagreeable *curmudgeon* long before he was awarded the Nobel Prize.

derisive

dih-RIH-siv

adj. contemptuous; mocking

The plaintiff who sought to have the words "under God" legally removed from the Pledge of Allegiance had such a *derisive* tone that his cause failed to garner many supporters.

diabolical

dy-uh-BOL-ik-ul

adj. outrageously wicked

Only the most *diabolical* villain could devise a plot using commercial jetliners to kill thousands of innocents.

discombobulated

dis-kum-BOB-yoo-lay-tid

v. to confuse or disconcert; upset; frustrate

When Lady Gaga appeared onstage at an awards show wearing a dress made entirely of steak, the spectacle certainly *discombobulated* the audience.

disputatious

dis-pyoo-TAY-shus

adj. prone to dispute; argumentative; contentious

Unless you are fond of frequent arguments, marry a **disputatious** spouse at your own peril.

dogmatic

dawg-MAT-ick

adj. given to arrogantly spouting opinions as if they were facts

The *New York Times'* **dogmatic** pro-amnesty, open-border stance has turned off many readers who oppose illegal immigration and has led to an avalanche of cancelled subscriptions.

dolosity

doh-LOSS-uh-tee

n. deceitfulness; hidden malice

Even some of President Obama's most ardent supporters want him to replace Attorney General Holder before the election, accusing the land's top law enforcement official of *dolosity*.

doltish

DOHLT-ish

adj. dull and stupid

I felt kind of **doltish** after getting every question wrong on the last Great American News Quiz.

doofus

DOO-fuss

n. a foolish or inept person

Only a *doofus* would squander all of his time on pointless diversions instead of working hard for a better life.

dumbledore

DUM-bul-dore

n. a busybody

J.K. Rowling named the headmaster in the Harry Potter books "Albus Dumbledore," perhaps considering him an actual *dumbledore* who got involved in everything.

dunderhead

DUN-durr-head

n. a dunce; a blockhead

Christian conservative groups consider the California state government to consist of a bunch of **dunderheads** after mandating that students be taught about gay history in the classroom.

enigma

uh-NIG-muh

n. a mystery; a perplexing situation

Asked about Russia, Churchill described the communist nation as "a riddle wrapped in a mystery inside an *enigma*."

equivocate

ee-KWIV-oh-kate

v. to prevaricate;
to use ambiguous language

Your humble correspondent will not hesitate
to chastise guests who opt to *equivocate*
rather than speak the no-spin truth.

eristic

ih-RISS-tick

adj. prone to contentious or questionable argument

We enjoy passionate and opinionated guests on The Factor, but keep it civil... no *eristic* behavior in the No Spin Zone, please!

exlex

EKS-leks

adj. beyond or outside the law

An *exlex*, not to be confused with a certain digestive medication, feels he or she is bound by no rules or laws.

fabulist

FAB-yoo-list

n. a liar; a person prone to telling tall tales

The author achieved wild success when Oprah made his biography part of her book club, but he was later discovered to be a *fabulist,* and his book was discredited.

fallacious

fuh-LAY-shus

adj. deceptive; misleading

When Democrats make their case for tax hikes for the wealthy, they use *fallacious* economic arguments to hide their true intention of income redistribution.

fandangle

fan-DANG-ull

n. garbage; rubbish

I was in no mood to put up with his ridiculous obfuscation and *fandangle*.

fatuous

FATCH-oo-us

adj. foolish or inane; silly

The president's zealous admirers treat even his most *fatuous* comments as if they were delivered by Zeus on a thunderbolt.

feckless

FECK-less

adj. incompetent; lazy; lacking in purpose

The Culture Warriors have tried, time and again, to explain what's behind the trend among *feckless* teens who text photos of themselves drinking and misbehaving.

fey

FAY

adj. whimsical; strange; otherworldly

People described as *fey* usually seem to be living in a different world—a world with just one slightly off-kilter inhabitant.

flapdoodle

FLAP-doo-dul

n. foolish talk; nonsense

One of The Factor's most popular segments is "Miller Time" because of Dennis' unique style that combines both insight and funny *flapdoodle*.

flummery

FLUM-uh-ree

n. complete nonsense

The debate over tax cuts overflowed with *flummery* and outright deceit on both sides.

flummoxed

FLUM-muxed

adj. confused; perplexed

Officials at the Berlin Zoo were ***flummoxed*** by the sudden death of their star polar bear Knut, who was relatively young when he collapsed.

foofaraw

FOO-fur-raw

n. a great fuss or disturbance about something very insignificant

Academic debates are marked by much *foofaraw* precisely because there is so little at stake.

fop

FOP

n. one who is excessively refined and vain

As you know, your humble correspondent isn't very interested in hob-nobbing with Hollywood *fops*; he is much more comfortable hanging with the regular folks.

fractious

FRAK-shus

adj. stubborn, difficult

As the crowd of Yankees fans grew louder and more *fractious*, the Bostonian wisely removed his Red Sox cap.

fuddy-duddy

FUD-ee-dud-ee

n. one who is stuffy, old-fashioned, and conservative

Despite his popular platform, the former governor's campaign for president failed to catch fire because voters perceived him as a ***fuddy-duddy*** who lacked charisma.

furciferous

fur-SIFF-ur-us

adj. scandalous; dishonorable; contemptible

Like Charles Ponzi before him, the *furciferous* Bernie Madoff created a cunning pyramid scheme.

furtive

FUR-tiv

adj. sly; shifty

During the debate, cameras caught the senator shooting a *furtive* glance at her advisor whenever her opponent botched an answer.

garrulous

GARE-yuh-luhs

adj. wordy or diffuse

After a couple of drinks, he turned
from verecund to talkative; a few more glasses,
and he was downright **garrulous**.

gasconading

gas-cuh-NEYD-ing

v. to boast extravagantly

After the soirée with the royal couple, there was plenty of *gasconading* amongst the party-goers about who got the most face time with the glamorous prince and duchess.

gnarly

NAR-lee

adj. difficult; nasty

The old guy with *gnarly* hands had a personality to match.

gongoozler

gon-GOOZ-lur

n. an idle spectator

Whether you agree or disagree with the tactics of the Minutemen, who have established armed watches at the Mexican border, you have to admire the fact that they're not *gongoozlers* when it comes to protecting the USA from rampant illegal immigrantion.

gormless

GORM-less

adj. stupid; lacking in intelligence

The reality show "Jersey Shore"
turned *gormless* clubbers into TV stars.

grame

GRAYME

n. hostility; anger

As *grame* builds in Syria, the U.S. State Department has struggled with defining its role in what is shaping up to be a civil war there.

grousing

GRAUS-ing

v. complaining; whining

It was late and there were no vacancies anywhere else, so *grousing* about the filthy hotel room would have been futile.

hackneyed

HACK-need

adj. commonplace or trite; stale

The *hackneyed* arguments to try the 9/11 ringleader in New York City civilian court didn't hold water, so the Obama administration changed its mind and opted for a military tribunal instead.

harangue

hur-RANG

v. to deliver a verbal attack

When a sitting president is taking questions from the press, he should be respectfully and thoroughly questioned, but reporters should not interrupt or *harangue* him.

harridan

HERR-uh-din

n. a hag; a shrew

The minority leader took umbrage when a member of the opposition party referred to her as a *harridan*.

honeyfuggle

HUN-ee-fug-gull

v. to dupe or deceive by flattery;
to obtain by deception

Sorry to bring him up again, but no one could
honeyfuggle a potential investor like Bernie Madoff could.

hooligan

HOO-li-guhn

n. a ruffian or hoodlum

The World Trade Organization conference in 1999 is best remembered for the band of angry *hooligans* who violently demonstrated in the streets of Seattle, causing millions of dollars' worth of damage.

hornswoggle

HORN-swog-gle

v. to swindle, cheat, hoodwink, or hoax

Selling the Brooklyn Bridge was once considered the ultimate *hornswoggle*, but now it may be a politician pledging to cut the budget deficit.

hotspur

HOT-spur

n. a hothead; an impetuous person

By attacking the deceased wife of her lover in her tell-all book, the politician's mistress came off as a spiteful *hotspur*.

hubris

HYOO-bris

n. excessive pride or arrogance

Even though our analysis of speculators' manipulation of oil prices has been spot on, Talking Points will refrain from displaying **hubris** if prices at the pump spike to reflect our theory.

imperious

im-PEER-ee-us

adj. domineering in a haughty manner; dictatorial

"I am in control here," declared the *imperious* Secretary of State.

impudent

IM-pyoo-dent

adj. disrespectful; insolent; contemptuous

Even some of Sarah Palin's staunchest critics found it *impudent* for the author who was writing a book about the former governor to buy the property next door to her family home in Alaska.

indolent

IN-doh-lent

adj. lazy; slothful

An entitlement state, with money taken from some folks and given to others, can lead people to be *indolent* and dependent.

insipid

in-SIP-id

adj. lacking any distinctive, interesting, or stimulating qualities

Actor Sean Penn is so *insipid* that he clamors for public attention by engaging in outlandish publicity stunts like meeting with the anti-American Venezuelan dictator Hugo Chavez.

insolent

IN-suh-lent

adj. disrespectful; insulting

Back when Bill was a high school teacher, a defiant student might be **insolent** once, but never twice!

insubordinate

in-suh-BOR-din-it

adj. disobedient

The quickest way to wind up in the stockade is to be *insubordinate* to your commanding officer.

invidious

in-VID-ee-us

adj. intended to create animosity
or resentment

The former candidate stormed off the set during a televised
interview because she found the line of questioning to be
invidious and insulting.

irascible

ih-RAS-uh-bul

adj. very angry or irritable

The imperious CEO grew *irascible* as the Congressional panel peppered him with what he felt were insolent questions.

jabberwocky

JAB-ur-wok-ee

n. nonsensical speech or writing; gibberish

When anti-American dictators are given a platform to speak to the world at the United Nations, it often turns into long-winded *jabberwocky* about the "evils" of the United States.

jackanapes

JACK-uh-napes

n. a presumptuous and impertinent person;
a whippersnapper

The Factor endeavors to explore all sides of the issues,
because only a *jackanapes* would refuse to consider opinions
aside from his or her own.

japery

JAYP-ur-ee

n. a joke; a mockery

The Harry Potter fanatics who dress in wizard gear and camp out for days to buy the latest book or see the latest movie must be a *japery*—don't they have anything better to do?

jejune

juh-JOON

adj. uninteresting; dull

The book was merely tedious,
but the movie adaptation was positively *jejune*.

jobation

joe-BAY-shun

n. a reprimand; a scolding

Democratic political pundits seem to think the Republican nominee deserves a *jobation* for working hard and accumulating personal wealth, but will voters agree?

jobbernowl

JOB-bur-nowl

n. a blockhead

Your humble correspondent assumed the rock star would be a *jobbernowl* who couldn't defend his outspoken radical political views; he was pleasantly surprised when the rocker was more than capable of intelligent and civil debate.

lemming

LEMM-ing

n. someone who follows the crowd without thinking

The ultimate *lemmings* were Jim Jones' followers, who followed him blindly and literally drank the poison-spiked Kool-Aid.

lethargic

luh-THAR-jik

adj. drowsy; sluggish

Murder charges against the single mother are forthcoming after she failed to seek medical attention for her sick and *lethargic* infant, which resulted in the baby's tragic death.

lilliputian

lil-i-PYOO-shun

adj. petty; trivial

Ronald Reagan had a way of making his opponents seem *liliputian* by comparison.

lily-livered

LILL-ee LIV-ered

adj. cowardly; timid

The *lily-livered* blogger who repeatedly attacked The Factor refused to come on the show to explain her beef, so we sent producer Jesse Watters to her!

loathsome

LOWTH-sum

adj. repulsive; disgusting

In the prison pecking order, child molesters
are considered the most *loathsome* of all criminals.

lollygagging

LOL-ee-gagg-ing

v. to spend time idly

I intended to create sentences for this book, but instead spent the day ***lollygagging***. Maybe tomorrow!

loogan

LOO-gun

n. an unsophisticated yokel

Not only had he never been to an airport, but the *loogan* boasted that he had never even ventured outside of his state or used a computer.

loquacious

loh-KWAY-shus

adj. characterized by excessive talk or wordiness

If you get too ***loquacious*** in answering questions in the No Spin Zone, Bill will ask you to get to the point, as The Factor is a fast-paced program; we don't have time to dawdle.

loutish

LOUT-ish

adj. boorish; ill-mannered

Poorly mannered to begin with, he grew more *loutish* with each additional whiskey and soda.

lugubrious

loo-GOO-bree-us

adj. mournful, dismal, or gloomy

When the ratings came out, the hallways of the low-rated cable network were filled with *lugubrious* expressions and a funereal atmosphere.

luminary

LOO-muh-ner-ee

n. a person who is inspirational to others

While many consider Al Gore a *luminary* for his work on behalf of the environment, questions have been raised about whether the high profits he's earned from his crusade make it a purely altruistic endeavor.

lusk

LUSK

n. a lazy person

With the unemployment rate so high and people across the country unable to find work, it's important to remember your friend or neighbor without a job is not necessarily a *lusk*!

malevolent

muh-LEV-uh-lent

adj. malicious; evil

The James Bond movies featured a series of extraordinary villains, each one more *malevolent* than the last.

martinet

mar-tin-ET

n. someone who stubbornly sticks to rules

The moderator of the presidential debate flustered the candidates by being a strict *martinet* when it came to time limits, often cutting the participants off mid-sentence.

maudlin

MAWD-lin

adj. foolishly sentimental

Some drunks get boisterous and cheery, while others grow *maudlin* and teary.

mawkish

MAWK-ish

adj. excessively and insincerely sentimental; falsely emotional

In front of the judge, the troubled young actress pretended to be contrite (but came off as completely *mawkish*) in order to win sympathy and a lenient sentence.

mendacious

men-DAY-shus

adj. lying; untruthful; dishonest

The defense team conceded that Casey Anthony was *mendacious* about everything, but insisted that lying doesn't make you a killer.

meretricious

mer-uh-TRISH-us

adj. gaudy; superficial; flashy

The beauty queen made the rounds on the talk show circuit, always wearing bright and *meretricious* attire to attract as much continued media attention as possible.

milquetoast

MILK-toast

adj. a spineless or timid person

The descriptive term "*milquetoast*" actually comes from an extremely wimpy comic strip character named Caspar Milquetoast.

minatory

MINN-uh-tore-ee

adj. threatening; dangerous

Deciding that discretion is the better part of valor, I crossed the street when a group of young men with an exceedingly *minatory* appearance approached from the other direction.

misanthrope

MIS-uhn-thrope

n. someone with an aversion to people and society

With their hatred of modernity and their criticism of humans, some environmentalists seem to be full-fledged *misanthropes*.

mischievous

MIS-chi-vus

adj. annoying; rogueish

Don't allow behavior that is merely *mischievous* to escalate into conduct that is malicious.

miscreant

MIS-kree-unt

n. an evildoer; a person without morals

After the mysterious disappearance of American teen Natalee Holloway in Aruba, a Dutch *miscreant* named Joran van der Sloot gained notoriety for his involvement in the case.

mooncalf

MOON-caff

n. a foolish person; an idle daydreamer

For a mendacious investment adviser, there is only one thing better than a *mooncalf*—a rich *mooncalf*.

mordant

MORE-dint

adj. sharply caustic or sarcastic

After Charlie Sheen's *mordant* diatribe against his "Two and a Half Men" producer, the troubled actor was fired from the sitcom and his popular character killed off in a bizarre freak accident.

morose

muh-ROHS

adj. gloomy; ill-humored

After being booted from office in a testy recall election, the disgraced governor grew *morose* and sullen.

mountebank

MOUN-tuh-bank

n. a quack

While researching doctors to repair his busted elbow, the Major League pitcher insisted on making sure he didn't end up with a *mountebank* as an orthopedist.

mugwump

MUG-wump

n. a person unable to make up his or her mind on an issue

As the Democratic candidate's position on gay marriage evolved to align with public opinion, there were growing accusations that his flip-flopping on social issues made him a *mugwump*.

murcid

MUR-sid

adj. lazy; slobbish

A good number of disability claims are being made by folks who are actually *murcid* malingerers.

namby-pamby

NAM-bee PAM-bee

n. a weak, insipid, cowardly person

Michele Bachmann, declaring that she is no ***namby-pamby***, boasted to Bill about her "titanium spine."

narcissistic

nar-suh-SIS-tick

adj. having a pronounced attachment to oneself

The career politician failed to connect with the American people on a human level because of his pretentious and *narcissistic* attitude.

ne'er-do-well

NAIR-do-well

n. one who is useless or good for nothing

Dennis Miller jokes that tattoos, now ubiquitous, were once the province of criminals and tough guys and *ne'er-do-wells*.

nebbish

NEBB-ish

n. a weak or timid person; a simpleton

Former classmates of the accused gunman recall the suspect as being a loner and a *nebbish*, a guy who rarely talked to anyone else and who didn't seem to have any friends.

nebulous

NEB-you-lus

adj. cloudy; unclear; hazy

The presidential candidate hypnotized crowds with his soaring rhetoric, even though his proposals were **nebulous** at best.

nefarious

ni-FAIR-ee-us

adj. extremely wicked

Only *nefarious* individuals with no moral compass would attempt to scam victims of natural disasters like tornadoes or earthquakes for their own personal gain.

neolithic

NEE-uh-lith-ik

adj. outdated; ancient

Elites in the mainstream media like to portray traditional Americans as backwards and *neolithic*.

nescience

NESS-ee-ence

n. a lack of knowledge; ignorance

Many skeptics think that only a person plagued with extreme *nescience* would get involved with a cult that is based on the teachings of a science fiction writer.

niding

NID-ding

n. a miserable, cheap, miserly person

The comedian Jack Benny, actually a very generous man, got laughs by depicting himself as a *niding*.

nimiety

ni-MAY-i-tee

n. an excess or overabundance

The debate about the estate tax was marked by a ***nimiety*** of socialistic rhetoric by the liberal commentator about the rich having to spread their wealth around to the less fortunate.

nimrod

NIM-rod

n. a person regarded as silly, foolish, or stupid

After decades of grade inflation, you'd have to be a *nimrod* or a lollygagger to flunk out of an Ivy League university.

ninnyhammer

NINN-ee-hamm-ur

n. a foolish person; a simpleton

A career criminal who robs the home of a police sergeant immediately after being released from prison is a *ninnyhammer* who deserves a few more years behind bars—and that's exactly what he'll get!

nitpick

NIT-pik

v. to criticize by focusing on inconsequential details

If your fiancée ignores all your inarguably superior features and constantly **nitpicks** at one teeny-tiny flaw, think twice about taking the plunge.

nitwit

NIT-wit

n. a slow-witted, stupid, or foolish person

Only a *nitwit* would set out to climb Mount Rainier in the middle of a blizzard; the end result will simply be hundreds of thousands of taxpayers' dollars spent on a futile rescue mission.

nixie

NICK-see

n. an undeliverable letter

Unless you type our email address correctly, your words of wisdom may find themselves in a pile of *nixies* somewhere in cyberspace.

noddy

NOD-ee

n. a foolish and silly person

Q: What's the difference between a nimrod,
a blatherskite, a mooncalf, and a *noddy*?
A: Not much; none of them can understand the question.

nudnik

NUHD-nick

n. a pesky or bothersome person

There is no punishment quite so cruel as being seated between two *nudniks* at a dinner party.

nugatory

NOO-guh-tor-ee

adj. having no real value; worthless

Because the liberal polling outfit tends to survey Americans who share its left-leaning opinions, its latest poll showing the Democratic incumbent as a heavy favorite is largely *nugatory*.

objurgate

OB-jer-gait

v. to berate sharply

The irascible actor lost his cool and proceeded to ***objurgate*** his 13-year-old daughter.

oblique

ub-LEEK

adj. not straight or direct

Economists were forecasting no improvement in the unemployment figures, while the administration was putting out *oblique* statistics showing job creation to calm the nation's fears.

obsequious

ub-SEE-kwee-us

adj. overly compliant or deferential

A competent CEO surrounds himself by independent thinkers, not *obsequious* lemmings.

obtuse

ub-TOOSE

adj. not quick or alert in perception, feeling, or intellect; dull

The heat blanketing the Northeast must be making some people *obtuse* because there was a real lack of energy at the recent town hall meetings about the economic downturn.

odious

OH-dee-us

adj. highly offensive; disgusting

The anti-war rally featured ***odious*** signs depicting the president as a latter-day Hitler.

oscitation

oss-uh-TAY-shun

n. the act of yawning

A page-turner like Killing Lincoln has been known to prevent the *oscitation* that often accompanies reading in bed late at night.

palter

PAWL-ter

v. to lie or use trickery

Martha Stewart's unwise decision to *palter* over her stock purchase resulted in a very public stint in a minimum-security prison.

parsimonious

par-suh-MOH-nee-us

adj. stingy; frugal; penny-pinching

His players accused the ***parsimonious*** team owner of tossing around nickels like they were manhole covers.

pawky

PAW-kee

adj. shrewd; cunning; sly

It was a ***pawky*** move for some in the Tea Party crowd to start circulating the idea of impeachment for the president if he didn't get the debt deal done in a timely fashion.

peccant

PEK-unt

adj. sinning; guilty of a moral offense

The Bible warns the *peccant* among us
to repent or face eternal damnation.

pecksniffian

peck-SNIFF-ee-un

adj. sanctimonious; falsely moralistic

The liberal pundit took a *pecksniffian* tone when arguing in favor of an amnesty plan, but the truth is that nobody is calling for mass deportations of otherwise law-abiding illegal immigrants.

pedagogue

PED-uh-gog

n. a dull and overly formal teacher or instructor

My high school history teacher was a *pedagogue* who never strayed from the assigned textbook.

pedantic

puh-DAN-tick

adj. overly concerned with minute details or formalisms

The more narrow and *pedantic* the teacher, the less inspired and creative the student.

pedestrian

puh-DES-tree-un

adj. lacking in imagination

The formula for many cable news programs has become so predictable and *pedestrian* that it's no wonder that more and more folks are turning to the Fox News Channel for something fresh and exciting.

peevish

PEE-vish

adj. showing a bad mood

The *peevish* hosts stormed off the set when a guest accurately pointed out that Muslims flew jetliners into the World Trade Center.

pejorative

pi-JOR-uh-tiv

adj. disparaging; belittling

As the bitter breakup of one of Hollywood's longest lasting couples descended into *pejorative* insults and accusations, the tabloid media worked itself up into a frenzy covering the sensational story.

perfidious

per-FID-ee-us

adj. deliberately faithless; treacherous; deceitful

He seemed pious and honest, but the preacher turned out to be as **perfidious** as Satan himself.

pernicious

per-NISH-us

adj. injurious; hurtful

British superstar Simon Cowell made a career out of *pernicious* critiques of aspiring young singers on the hit show "American Idol."

persnickety

per-SNICK-i-tee

adj. overparticular; fussy or snobish

Many rock stars are notorious for their *persnickety* demands about precisely what must be in their dressing rooms.

perspicacious

pur-spi-KAY-shus

adj. having keen perception and understanding; discerning

In the talk show host's first sit-down interview with the former presidential candidate, he found her to have an exceedingly *perspicacious* mind when it came to analyzing complex issues.

pestiferous

pes-TIFF-ur-us

adj. annoying; bothersome; irritating

Tsetse flies can be deadly; houseflies are merely ***pestiferous***.

pettifogger

PET-ee-fah-gur

n. someone who uses petty and unscrupulous tactics

While some have labeled the disgruntled flight attendant a *pettifogger* for escaping his plane via the emergency slide while on the tarmac, others fully understood his frustration and supported his antics.

petulant

PET-yoo-lunt

adj. showing sudden, impatient irritation

The *petulant* child screamed and wailed inconsolably when he was told that he couldn't have any ice cream prior to dinner.

philistine

FIL-uh-steen

adj. lacking in, or hostile to, culture

Philistine attitudes abound amongst American teenagers who seem to favor wasting time with video games and electronics over more worthwhile endeavors like reading.

picayune

pick-uh-YOON

adj. of little value or importance; petty

The Picayune was a Spanish coin with very little value; not surprisingly, the word "*picayune*" is synonymous with insignificance and triviality.

pinhead

PIN-head

n. a stupid person; nitwit

If you hurt children, betray the United States, or defame innocent people, you will automatically be branded a *pinhead* for life in the No Spin Zone.

pithy

PITH-ee

adj. brief and meaningful

As everyone knows, letters are far more likely to be read if they are *pithy* and pointed, not wordy and nebulous.

plonker

PLONK-ur

n. a dolt; a stupid person

If you have delayed in buying yourself one of our nifty "Restore the USA" doormats, you just may be a ***plonker***!

pollrumptious

pole-RUMP-shus

adj. overconfident; unruly

The aforementioned Caspar Milquetoast was always timid and never ***pollrumptious***.

poltroon

pole-TROON

n. a spineless coward

The Internet seems to be full of **poltroons** who delight in hurling insults and invective—but only when they can remain anonymous behind their keyboards.

polymath

POL-ee-math

n. an expert in several often divergent fields of study

In selecting a running mate, it is wise for a presidential nominee to choose a well-rounded *polymath* whose varied expertise will bring value to the ticket.

popinjay

POP-in-jay

n. a vain and overly talkative person; a chatterbox

I got stuck next to a *popinjay* who spent the entire flight combing his hair and talking about jejune subjects.

porcine

pour-SEEN

adj. resembling a swine; piggish

The gluttonous and ***porcine*** Mr. Creosote from the Monty Python movie "The Meaning of Life" met a disgusting demise when he couldn't stop himself from overindulging.

priggish

PRIG-gish

adj. demands pointlessly precise conformity

The mighty British Empire was, in effect, run by overly proper and *priggish* civil servants who slavishly enforced every rule.

procacity

pro-CASS-ih-tee

n. forwardness; petulance

In the business of entertainment reporting, a temperament marked by **procacity** and assertiveness is beneficial when trying to nab red carpet interviews with in-demand celebrities.

procrustean

pro-KRUS-tee-un

adj. designed to produce conformity using violence

Labor bosses despise the secret ballot; they prefer a *procrustean* "card check" system that would pressure workers to endorse a union.

prudish

PROO-dish

adj. excessively proper or modest in speech

The "Church Lady," Dana Carvey's character from "Saturday Night Live," is a pitch-perfect parody of *prudish* tastes taken to their extremes.

puerile

PYOOR-ile

adj. childishly foolish; immature or trivial

Most of the Bush-bashing bumper stickers were *puerile*, totally lacking in sophistication or humor.

pugnacious

pug-NAY-shus

adj. combative; belligerent

Though the two men are said to be fond of each other personally, the exchanges between John McCain and Barack Obama during their run for the White House had a tendency to get a bit hostile and *pugnacious*.

puzzlewit

PUHZ-ul-wit

n. a stupid, dimwitted person

Ironically, a *puzzlewit* can't solve a simple puzzle…
and has absolutely no wit.

quakebuttock

KWAYK-butt-uck

n. a sniveling coward

The Somali pirate sure acted brave while he was armed with an AK-47, but he quickly turned into a *quakebuttock* once he entered the courtroom to face charges.

querulous

KWER-yoo-lus

adj. full of complaints

The day after the wedding, she went from agreeable to *querulous*, complaining about everything from his clothing to his snoring.

quidnunc

KWID-nunk

n. a person who is eager to know the latest news and gossip; busybody

The Congressman has proven himself to be a real *quidnunc*, more interested in trafficking in Beltway gossip than in working to solve his constituents' problems.

quixotic

kwik-SOT-ic

adj. unpredictable; resembling Don Quixote

At first blush, it seemed ***quixotic*** that a first-term senator with no executive experience would run for the White House.

rambunctious

ram-BUNK-shus

adj. difficult to control or handle; wildly boisterous

Rambunctious hockey fans in Canada reacted to their team's tough loss by rioting in the streets, prompting police to use rubber bullets and tear gas to get the crowd under control.

rapscallion

rap-SKAL-yun

n. a rascal; a rogue

Much of his wayward youth was spent in a pool room hanging around with drunks, thieves and assorted *rapscallions*.

recalcitrant

ree-KALSE-uh-trant

adj. stubborn; defiant

The lingering debt deadlock was marked by *recalcitrant* politicians on both sides of the aisle whorefused to compromise on the best interests of the country.

restive

RESS-tiv

adj. edgy; tense; jittery

The crowd was **restive** to begin with, but the firebrand's speech pushed them over the edge.

sagacious

suh-GAY-shus

adj. acutely insightful and wise

Strict constitutionalists believe the Founding Fathers were *sagacious* men whose writings were timeless and whose values still apply today.

sapid

SAP-id

adj. agreeable; to one's liking

Great food is **sapid** to the taste buds, great literature **sapid** to the mind, and great Factor gear **sapid** to the eyes.

sardonic

sar-DON-ick

adj. cynical; bitter

His **sardonic** comments, while delivered with a grin, seemed to betray an intense underlying anger.

saturnine

SAT-ur-nine

adj. bitter; gloomy; surly

The mood in the politician's office was *saturnine* following his televised admission that he had in fact engaged in inappropriate behavior on the Internet.

sawder

SAW-dur

v. to flatter; to overtly praise

Political conventions have become nothing more than dog-and-pony shows where the party faithful *sawder* their nominee—no real decisions are made.

scelestious

skuh-LESS-tee-us

adj. wicked or evil

One challenge for young Harry Potter was discerning which wizards were righteous and which were *scelestious*.

scurrilous

SKURR-uh-lus

adj. coarse; jocular; derisive

The newspaper's ombudsman had some choice words for the opinion columnist whose previous article had contained shockingly **scurrilous** invective aimed at a minority group.

skullduggery

skul-DUG-uh-ree

n. trickery; underhandedness

With President Nixon cruising toward an easy re-election, there was no need for his "plumbers" to resort to *skullduggery*.

snarky

SNAR-kee

adj. testy or irritable; short

After leaving the White House, Bill Clinton has sometimes gotten very *snarky* when asked about the Monica Lewinsky scandal that led to his historic impeachment.

snippy

SNIP-ee

adj. sharp or curt

When the candidates started bickering on the phone about the Florida results, Gore demanded that Bush stop being so *snippy*.

snollygoster

SNOLL-ee-gos-tur

n. a shrewd, clever, unscrupulous individual

The *snollygosters* in the New Black Panthers who stood outside a polling place in 2008 waving billy clubs were never prosecuted for voter intimidation, but they should have been.

somnambulant

som-NAM-byoo-lent

n., adj. a sleepwalker; one who sleepwalks

Medical experts were baffled when they learned that some users of prescription sleep aids engage in *somnambulant* feasts, sometimes even gorging on inedible or toxic substances.

sop

SOP

n. a weak-willed or spineless person

Michael Jackson supporters deny the pop star would ever have harmed a child, and say the molestation charges against him were made by a *sop* looking to cash in on her son's friendship with the international star.

sophist

SOF-ist

n. a person who uses elaborate
and deceptive arguments

It took a truly skilled *sophist* to convince a jury that the
comely mom did not kill her infant daughter.

splenetic

spluh-NET-ick

adj. crabby; irritable; spiteful

The classic interrogation technique involves a patient and understanding cop teamed with a *splenetic* and impatient partner.

spurious

SPYOOR-ee-us

adj. not genuine, authentic, or true; counterfeit

After Osama bin Laden was discovered hunkered down near a military complex in Pakistan, many Americans wondered if the alliance between our country and theirs was *spurious*.

superbious

soo-PURB-ee-us

adj. proud; arrogant; overbearing

Some fans felt LeBron James was *superbious* when he staged a TV spectacular to announce his decision to play for Miami.

supercilious

soo-per-SILL-ee-us

adj. showing arrogance, superiority or haughtiness

President Nixon's initial refusal to release the Watergate tapes to a Senate committee, claiming they were vital to national security, was a *supercilious* move for which he was harshly judged by the American public.

surly

SUR-lee

adj. unfriendly or hostile

TSA agents are almost uniformly cordial, but we've all run into a few *surly* ones as well.

sycophant

SICK-oh-fant

n. a flatterer; a fawning parasite

Powerful people like Oprah Winfrey have to be extra cautious not to surround themselves with *sycophants* who don't really have their best interests at heart.

tedious

TEE-dee-us

adj. long, tiresome and boring

I left my copy of *Killing Lincoln* at home, making the flight all the more ***tedious***.

temerity

tuh-MER-i-tee

n. recklessness; rashness

Refusing to heed tsunami warnings by not seeking shelter on higher ground is a sign of *temerity* that can have deadly consequences.

temulent

TIM-yoo-lent

adj. drunk or intoxicated

Lots of folks suspect Charlie Sheen was *temulent* when he sat down for a series of bizarre television interviews.

tendentious

ten-DEN-shus

adj. opinionated; biased; partisan

The Factor tries to avoid giving a platform to *tendentious* individuals who stick to partisan talking points and refuse to listen to reason.

tenebrific

ten-uh-BRIFF-ick

adj. gloomy; dark

As the votes were being tallied, a *tenebrific* air settled over the campaign's headquarters as it became obvious that it was now mathematically impossible for the candidate to win.

tenuous

TEN-yoo-uhs

adj. lacking in clarity; vague

Keynesians say more government spending leads to more employment, but the link between the two is *tenuous* at best.

terse

TURSE

adj. succinct, to the point; brusque

George Washington's *terse* inaugural address in 1793, in which he simply expressed his commitment to the Oath of Office, was the shortest in presidential history.

thewless

THEW-less

adj. lacking in energy

Answer: The shoeless, clueless, and *thewless*.
Question: Who is barefoot, dumb, and lethargic?

troglodyte

TROG-luh-dyte

n. a secluded person who is unfamiliar with the world

Perhaps the American election system should be revamped to compensate for the *troglodytes* who cast votes for whichever candidate the mainstream media throws its weight behind.

truculent

TRUCK-you-lent

adj. eager to fight; defiant

The mustachioed immigration advocate entered the No Spin Zone in a *truculent* mood and promptly got the fight he was seeking.

unctuous

UNK-choo-us

adj. excessively smug

The professional athlete's ***unctuous*** refusal of a multimillion dollar contract didn't sit well with fans of the game who already think the players are overpaid.

vacillate

VASS-uh-late

v. to waver in mind or opinion;
to be indecisive

Depending on the audience, an obsequious politician can *vacillate* between advocating fiscal discipline and promising new spending.

vacuous

VACK-you-us

adj. lacking in ideas or intelligence; vapid

It was shocking to see the usually *vacuous* starlet featured in a thoughtful, poignant PSA about the need for respectful dissent in debates about social issues among Americans.

vainglorious

veyn-GLOR-ee-us

adj. characterized by or exhibiting vanity; boastful

The most dangerous place to stand is between a *vainglorious* man and a mirror.

varlet

VAR-let

n. a rogue; a deceitful scoundrel

Most Americans are fed up with back-room politics being conducted by *varlets* whose primary concern is whether they'll get sent back to Washington in their next election.

venomous

VEN-uh-muhs

adj. spiteful; malignant

Loony left-wingers seem to unleash their most *venomous* attacks on female conservatives.

verbose

vur-BOSE

adj. overly wordy

Don't give your humble correspondent a headache by sending ***verbose*** letters—you've got to keep it pithy!

verecund

VER-i-kund

adj. modest; shy

It's not uncommon for a *verecund* child to blossom into a confident and extroverted adult.

vexation

veck-SAY-shun

n. the state of being irritated or annoyed

There was excessive *vexation* in Chicago
after a Cubs fan interfered with a ball in play,
leading to the team's painful loss in the playoffs.

vilipend

VIL-uh-pend

v. to vilify; to belittle

Some observers believe our political decline began in 1987 when Ted Kennedy took to the Senate floor to **vilipend** Judge Robert Bork.

virago

vi-RAH-goh

n. a scold; a nag

Critics of Michelle Obama's anti-obesity campaign accuse the First Lady of acting like a *virago*, telling Americans what they can and cannot eat.

visigoth

VIZ-i-goth

n. a barbarian

The swells in Garden City loathed kids from Levittown, viewing them as nothing more than a bunch of crude *visigoths*.

vitriolic

vit-ree-OLL-ick

adj. scathing; angry; hateful

The left-wing attacks on President George W. Bush grew even more *vitriolic* during his second term in office.

vituperative

vie-TOO-pur-uh-tiv

adj. characterized by abusive language

Friends of O.J. and Nicole Brown Simpson often worried about her safety because of the overly *vituperative* nature of their very public fights.

vociferous

vo-SIFF-ur-us

adj. loud; noisy

Nothing can spoil a movie
quite like a bunch of *vociferous* teens.

wisenheimer

WY-zen-hy-mur

n. wiseacre or smart aleck

During his bitter dispute with NBC about whether he would continue hosting "The Tonight Show," *wisenheimer* Conan O'Brien took to the airwaves with some nasty jokes about his employer.

yawping

YAWP-ing

v. the act of making loud cries;
to complain loudly

We'd rather not hear any *yawping* about the fact that
this is the 250th and final word
in the second edition of *Factor Words*!